¡Es Navid[ad!]

por Richard Sebra

EDICIONES LERNER ◆ MINEÁPOLIS

Muchas gracias a José Becerra-Cárdenas, maestro de segundo grado en Little Canada Elementary, por revisar este libro.

Nota a los educadores:
A través de este libro encontrarán preguntas para el pensamiento crítico. Estas preguntas pueden utilizarse para hacer que los lectores jóvenes piensen críticamente del tema con la ayuda del texto y las imágenes.

La traducción al español fue realizada por Giessi Lopez.

ediciones Lerner
Una división de Lerner Publishing Group, Inc.
241 First Avenue North
Mineápolis, MN 55401, EE. UU.

Si desea averiguar acerca de niveles de lectura y para obtener más información, favor consultar este título en www.lernerbooks.com

Library of Congress Cataloging-in-Publication Data

Names: Sebra, Richard, 1984– author.
Title: ¡Es Navidad! / por Richard Sebra.
Other titles: It's Christmas! Spanish
Description: Minneapolis : Ediciones Lerner, 2018. | Series: Bumba books en español. ¡es una fiesta! | Includes bibliographical references and index. | Audience: Age 4–7. | Audience: K to grade 3.
Identifiers: LCCN 2017053129 (print) | LCCN 2017056162 (ebook) | ISBN 9781541507869 (eb pdf) | ISBN 9781541503441 (lb : alk. paper) | ISBN 9781541526587 (pb : alk. paper)
Subjects: LCSH: Christmas—Juvenile literature.
Classification: LCC GT4985.5 (ebook) | LCC GT4985.5 .S4318 2018 (print) | DDC 394.2663—dc23

LC record available at https://lccn.loc.gov/2017053129

Fabricado en los Estados Unidos de América
1-43839-33672-1/3/2018

Tabla de contenido

Época Navideña

La Navidad es una fiesta alegre.

La gente la celebra alrededor del mundo.

La celebración es en el invierno.

Es el 25 de diciembre.

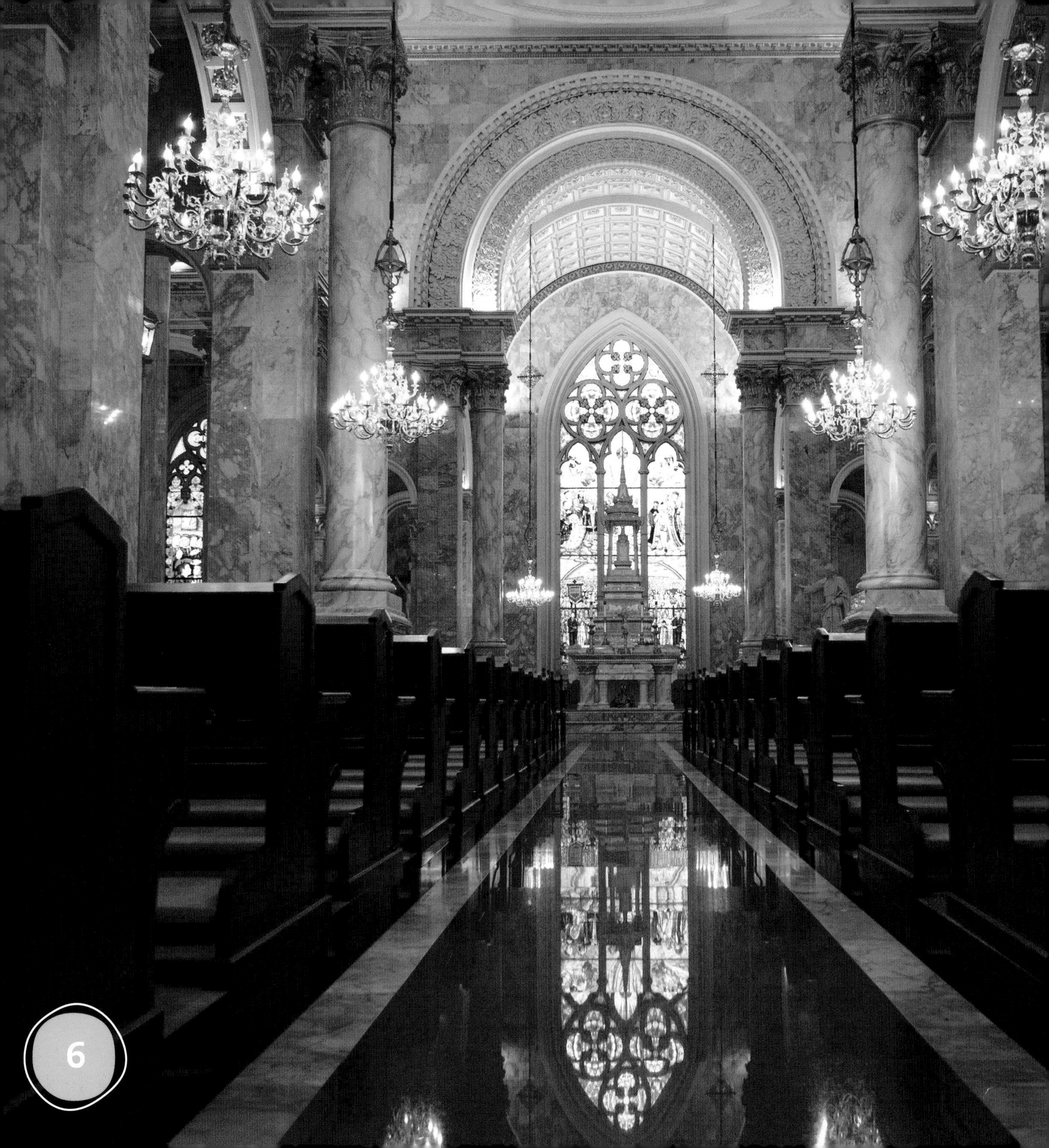

La Navidad es una

fiesta cristiana.

Muchas personas van

a la iglesia.

La gente decora sus casas.

Cuelgan luces.

Cuelgan también coronas navideñas.

¿De qué otra manera pueden las personas decorar su casa?

corona
navideña

adorno
navideño

Las personas ponen árboles de Navidad en sus casas.

Los árboles son bonitos.

Tienen muchas luces.

Tienen muchos adornos navideños.

Las familias se reúnen.

Comen grandes comidas.

Muchas familias comen

jamón o pavo.

Las galletas son

de postre.

Las personas se dan regalos los unos a los otros. Los regalos son envueltos en papel. Los niños por lo regular reciben juguetes.

¿Qué otros regalos pueden recibir los niños?

La gente canta villancicos navideños.

Algunas personas cantan para sus vecinos.

Muchas personas escriben tarjetas de Navidad. Le envían las tarjetas a sus amistades. Escriben de los sucesos del año anterior.

¿Qué escribirías en una tarjeta de Navidad?

La Navidad es una época
de alegría.
Es un tiempo de celebración.

Calendario Navideño

Algunas personas usan calendarios especiales para contar los días hasta Navidad.

Glosario de imágenes

adornos navideños

cosas lindas que se le ponen al árbol de Navidad

coronas navideñas

círculos de hojas o flores

iglesia

un lugar donde la gente ora

regalos

artículos que las personas se dan en una fiesta

Índice

Leer más

Felix, Rebecca. *We Celebrate Christmas in Winter*. Ann Arbor, MI: Cherry Lake Publishing, 2014.

Pettiford, Rebecca. *Christmas*. Minneapolis: Jump!, 2015.

Stevens, Kathryn. *Christmas Trees*. Mankato, MN: The Child's World, 2015.

Agradecimientos de imágenes

Las imágenes en este libro son utilizadas con el permiso de: © Torwai Seubsri/Shutterstock.com, página 5; © a454/Shutterstock.com, páginas 6–7, 23 (arriba a la izquierda); © quackersnaps/iStock.com, páginas 9, 23 (abajo a la derecha); © EarnestTse/iStock.com, páginas 10, 23 (abajo a la izquierda); © Monkey Business Images/Shutterstock.com, páginas 12–13, 18; © oliveromg/Shutterstock.com, páginas 14, 23 (arriba a la derecha); © Juanmonino/iStock.com, páginas 16–17; © monkeybusinessimages/iStock.com, página 21; © evemilla/iStock.com, página 22.

Portada: © RoJo.com/Shutterstock.com.

Animal Offspring

Cows and Their Calves

by Margaret Hall

Consulting Editor: Gail Saunders-Smith, Ph.D.

Consultant: Steven Stewart, DVM
College of Veterinary Medicine, University of Minnesota
St. Paul, Minnesota

Capstone press®
Mankato, Minnesota

Pebble Plus is published by Capstone Press
1710 Roe Crest Drive, North Mankato, Minnesota 56003
www.capstonepub.com

Books published by Capstone Press are manufactured with paper containing at least 10 percent post-consumer waste.

Library of Congress Cataloging-in-Publication Data
Hall, Margaret, 1947–
Cows and their calves / by Margaret Hall.
v. cm.—(Pebble plus: Animal offspring)
Includes bibliographical references (p. 23) and index.
Contents: Cows—A calf—Growing up—Watch cows grow.
ISBN-13: 978-0-7368-2105-6 (hardcover)
ISBN-10: 0-7368-2105-8 (hardcover)
ISBN-13: 978-0-7368-4644-8 (softcover pbk.)
ISBN-10: 0-7368-4644-1 (softcover pbk.)
1. Calves—Juvenile literature. 2. Cows—Juvenile literature. [1. Cows. 2. Animals—Infancy.] I. Title. II. Series.
SF205 .H26 2004
636.2'07—dc21 2002155598

Editorial Credits
Sarah L. Schuette, editor; Kia Adams, series designer; Jennifer Schonborn, cover production designer; Kelly Garvin, photo researcher; Eric Kudalis, product planning editor

Photo Credits
Bruce Coleman Inc./Hans Reinhard, 13; Lynn Stone, 21 (right)
Index Stock Imagery/Lynn Stone, cover
Minden Pictures/Yva Momatiuk/John Eastcott, 1, 21 (left); Mitsuaki Iwago, 4–5; Jim Brandenburg, 18–19
PhotoDisc Inc., 20 (both)
Tom Stack & Associates/Bob Pool, 17; Joe McDonald, 10–11
Visuals Unlimited/Inga Spence, 7, 9; Patrick J. Endres, 14–15

Note to Parents and Teachers

The Animal Offspring series supports national science standards related to life science. This book describes and illustrates cows and their calves. The images support early readers in understanding the text. The repetition of words and phrases helps early readers learn new words. This book also introduces early readers to subject-specific vocabulary words, which are defined in the Glossary section. Early readers may need assistance to read some words and to use the Table of Contents, Glossary, Read More, Internet Sites, and Index/Word List sections of the book.

Word Count: 109
Early-Intervention Level: 12

Printed in the United States of America in Eau Claire, Wisconsin.
102013
007809R

Table of Contents

Cows

Cows are mammals. Cows have black, brown, white, or red hair. Young cows are called calves.

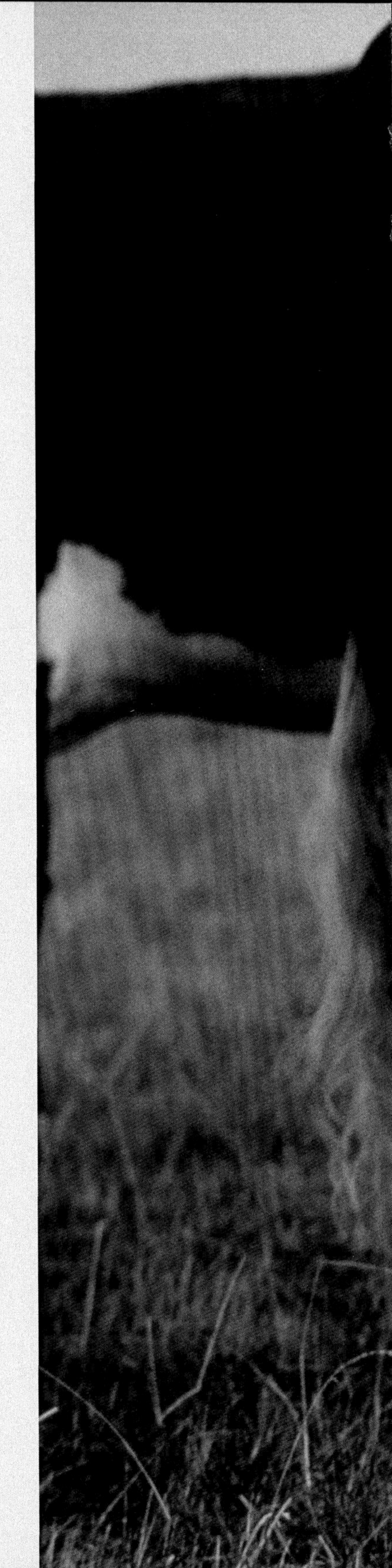

Cows and calves graze in pastures on farms and ranches. Cows and calves sometimes live in barns.

A male is a bull. A female is a cow. Bulls and cows mate. A calf begins to grow inside the cow.

The Calf

The cow gives birth to a calf. The cow takes care of the calf.

Calves have long legs. Calves can stand up about one hour after they are born.

Calves drink milk from their mothers.

Growing Up

Calves start to eat hay, grass, and grain after about one month.

Calves become adults after about two years.

Watch Cows Grow

birth

adult after about
two years

Glossary

birth—the event of being born; cows usually give birth to one calf at a time; cows sometimes have twins.

bull—an adult male of the cattle family; bulls can father young; male calves that do not become fathers are called steers.

cow—an adult female of the cattle family; a young cow is called a heifer before she gives birth to a calf for the first time.

graze—to eat grass and other plants that are growing in a pasture or field

mammal—a warm-blooded animal that has a backbone and hair or fur; female mammals feed milk to their young.

mate—to join together to produce young; cows give birth nine months after mating.

pasture—land that animals use to graze

Read More

Murphy, Andy. *Out and About at the Dairy Farm.* Minneapolis: Picture Window Books, 2003.

Powell, Jillian. *From Calf to Cow.* How Do They Grow? Austin, Texas: Raintree Steck-Vaughn, 2001.

Taus-Bolstad, Stacy. *From Grass to Milk.* Start to Finish. Minneapolis: Lerner, 2003.

Trumbauer, Lisa. *The Life Cycle of a Cow.* Life Cycles. Mankato, Minn.: Pebble Books, 2003.

Internet Sites

Do you want to find out more about cows and their calves? Let FactHound, our fact-finding hound dog, do the research for you.

Here's how:

1) Visit ***http://www.facthound.com***

2) Type in the **Book ID** number: **0736821058**

3) Click on **FETCH IT**.

FactHound will fetch Internet sites picked by our editors just for you!

Index/Word List